For Mia —MB

For my children: Klara, Nina, Kristina, and Gabriel —RI

About This Book

The illustrations for this book were done in oil paint on canvas. This book was edited by Nikki Garcia and designed by Brenda E. Angelilli. The production was supervised by Patricia Alvarado, and the production editors were Jen Graham and Esther Reisberg. The text was set in Mrs Eaves OT, and the display type is Myster Text.

Doña Fela's Dream

Written by Monica Brown

Illustrated by Rosa Ibarra

L B

Little, Brown and Company

New York   Boston

The people of La Perla were scared. The winds blew fiercely, and dark clouds swirled in the sky. A tropical storm headed toward the island of Puerto Rico. The villagers' barrio was made up of shacks that hugged the cliffs outside the walls of Old San Juan.

What if their homes fell into the sea? Where could they go? Who could they turn to? There was only one place they could count on.

Families gathered in the streets and walked toward Doña Fela's house. With braids in her hair and a flower behind her ear, Doña Fela answered their knock.

"Come in, all of you!" Doña Fela said. "Dry off, and I will make you something to eat."

More people turned to Doña Fela, who opened her
doors to all, until finally there was no more space or food.
Still, local officials refused to open a shelter.

"Then I will do it myself!" she said, breaking down the
doors of a local school.

Doña Fela saved many lives that day, and the sanjuaneros asked her to become their mayor. "San Juan needs you!" they said. But there had never been a female mayor of San Juan before.

Felisa was born when women weren't allowed to vote and most couldn't read or write.

Felisa's father believed that women had no place in politics and that it was up to the men to solve Puerto Rico's problems. But even as a young girl, Felisa disagreed.

Felisa saw injustice all over the island—from prejudice against Black Puerto Ricans to the treatment of jíbaros, the country people who worked the land and barely earned enough to feed their children.

She wondered why some families, like her own, had so much and others so little.

Felisa believed the workers should share in the harvest.

And then a great heartbreak came to the Rincón family. Felisa's mother—her first and most important teacher—died during childbirth.

Felisa left school to help raise her younger siblings, giving up her dreams for her family. Her brothers and sisters knew to behave when they smelled jasmine, because it meant that their big sister, who always wore flowers in her hair, was nearby.

And each day, Felisa woke up before the sun to make café
y pan for her family's workers, as well as for the jíbaros passing
the Rincón farm on their way to the big sugar plantations.

Puerto Rican women who could read and write gained the right to vote in 1929, and a new dream bloomed in Felisa's heart, like a Flor de Maga in the sun. Felisa told her father that she was going to register to vote.

"No!" he said once again. "Women have no place in politics!"

"Yes!" she said, disobeying him. "If I have this right, I'm going to use it."

There was no changing Felisa's mind, so Felisa's father walked alongside her to the city center.

Felisa was the fifth woman on the island to register to vote, and on that day she vowed to be a voice for change. She knew that the people of Puerto Rico deserved better, so she became a political organizer, soon growing into a trusted leader.

Felisa joined the Liberal Party and recruited voters—especially women—in the poorest neighborhoods of San Juan, including La Perla, where there was no fresh water. No one had ever listened as carefully to their needs as the woman with flowers in her hair.

She became known as Doña Fela, and together with another politician, she helped a new political party take root—the Popular Democratic Party. Doña Fela helped spread the message of "Pan, Tierra y Libertad!"

Doña Fela met another organizer, a lawyer named Genaro Gautier, and they fell in love. They married and worked side by side, but like her father, Felisa's new husband didn't think a woman should become mayor.

Doña Fela obeyed at first . . . until the tropical storm brought frightened sanjuaneros to her door. *Is now the time?* she wondered.

She thought all night of the gray sky, the fierce wind, the unprotected children, and the rain that wouldn't stop. Together, they survived the night.

And by the time the sun finally came out the next day, Doña Fela had made a decision. "I will become mayor, because I want the power to help people," she said.

And that is exactly what she did. In office, Doña Fela blossomed. She was a whirlwind of work, bringing fresh water to La Perla and other poor neighborhoods, buying new garbage trucks to clean up the city,

building affordable housing,

and saving buildings in Old San Juan from ruin.

Doña Fela wanted all Puerto Rican children to learn, so she established the first preschools on the island, called escuelas maternales. She hired teachers from the barrios and trained them herself.

Doña Fela planted seeds of change and watched the children of San Juan flower.

Many in government thought that some problems were too large to solve. But not Doña Fela!

Every Wednesday, she opened the city hall doors to the residents of San Juan, and it became known as the People's House. She tackled problems, one by one, big and small.

Doña Fela helped sanjuaneros when they struggled, and celebrated with them when they were happy. She sang and danced, leading many festivals and joining her people in the sea on the Noche de San Juan.

The sea washed away all sadness and left only hope behind.

The mayor wanted the children of her city to know every natural wonder—even snow!

A plane full of snow flew to the city of San Juan. For the first time, children of the tropics had snowball fights, built snowmen, and dived into huge piles of snow.

The air rang with the sounds of their laughter and joy.

Doña Fela's fame grew around the world, and presidents and politicians sought her advice and honored her with awards.

She was known for her hard work, compassion, imagination, and flair in solving the city's problems.

She was recognized everywhere she went because of the flutter of the Spanish fan in her hand, the thick braids wrapped around her head, and of course, the flowers in her hair.

Doña Fela, alcaldesa, believed it was love, not just politics, that got things done. The people of San Juan loved her, and she loved them back. She won every election and served as mayor for decades. . . .

And she taught every child in Puerto Rico that, in the sunlight
that comes after the rain, flowering dreams can grow.

AUTHOR'S NOTE

Before there were Supreme Court Justice Sonia Sotomayor, San Juan Mayor Carmen Yulín Cruz, and US Representatives Nydia Velázquez and Alexandria Ocasio-Cortez, there was Felisa Rincón de Gautier. Affectionately called Doña Fela by her constituents, she was the first female mayor of San Juan, Puerto Rico, and the first female mayor of any capital city in the Américas. Her tenure as mayor was marked by her dedication to the well-being of children and the poor.

Felisa was born on January 9, 1897, in the town of Ceiba, Puerto Rico—the island known as Borinquen by the Indigenous Taínos who inhabited it first. After over four hundred years of Spanish colonial rule, Puerto Rico came under the control of the United States. Felisa's father supported Puerto Rican independence, and his political passions shaped Felisa's childhood, despite the many restrictions placed on girls and women in this era. Felisa was a dutiful and obedient daughter—to an extent. Against her father's explicit wishes, she registered to vote and joined the Liberal Party. She was an active member, becoming a political organizer in the poorest neighborhoods of San Juan. One of her greatest political gifts was her ability to listen and connect to people, motivated by compassion and a commitment to social justice.

When Luis Muñoz Marín left the Liberal Party, Felisa joined him in establishing the Popular Democratic Party of Puerto Rico. Like Muñoz Marín, Doña Fela wanted to preserve the language and culture of Puerto Rico but draw upon what she felt were great economic benefits that came from its association with the United States. She was appointed mayor in 1947 and decisively won four subsequent elections.

Doña Fela's love of fashion and flowers as self-expression was iconic, and the beloved mayor leveraged her popularity and political influence in the service of San Juan's citizens. She brought health clinics, running water, better sanitation, and legal aid offices to the most distressed neighborhoods in Puerto Rico, and her escuelas maternales became the model for Head Start programs in the United States.

Hundreds of thousands of people relied on Doña Fela, and she took this responsibility seriously. Yet she never lost her sense of joy, individuality, or the importance of celebrating with her community.

Doña Fela became an international star and one of the most powerful political figures on the island. She was a favorite of presidents and politicians and represented the United States and Puerto Rico all over the world. Even after she stepped down as mayor at the age of

AUTHOR'S NOTE (CONTINUED)

seventy, she continued to be deeply involved in politics, serving as a Goodwill Ambassador in South America, Europe, and Asia, and as a member of the Democratic National Committee, receiving many awards for her service. She died on September 16, 1994, at the age of ninety-seven. Just two years earlier, at ninety-five years old, she was the oldest delegate ever to attend the Democratic National Convention.

Today, if you were to walk through the bright red gate at the Puerto de San Juan with the sea at your back, you would look up and see the rose-pink house that was once Doña Fela's. On the house is a sign for the Casa Museo Felisa Rincón de Gautier. It is now a museum honoring her life's work.

Go inside and visit the paintings and photos and the many awards that line the walls. See the dresses and the fans and the dolls. Imagine your life as you learn about hers, and remember that Doña Fela, alcaldesa, taught us to listen, to be joyful, and to always strive for justice.

Doña Fela kisses a baby during a tour of a poor neighborhood.

GLOSSARY

alcaldesa . . . . mayor (fem.)

barrio . . . . neighborhood

café y pan . . . . coffee and bread

doña . . . . title given to a woman of rank

escuelas maternales . . . . preschools

Flor de Maga . . . . Maga flower

jíbaro . . . . rural Puerto Rican farmer,
                                  laborer

Noche de
San Juan . . . . Eve of the Feast of San Juan

Pan, Tierra y
Libertad . . . . Bread, Land, and Freedom

sanjuaneros . . . . those born in, or longtime
                                  residents of, San Juan

ARTIST'S NOTE

My childhood in Puerto Rico was full of joy and adventure. Our family lived in Old San Juan, on Caleta de las Monjas. I have such fond memories of running through the streets of the old city with my siblings and friends; playing near La Fortaleza, the governor's house; and eating limbers, a Puerto Rican–style ice cream, and piraguas, a frozen treat made of shaved ice and fruit-flavored syrup.

Doña Fela lived on Caleta de San Juan, one street over from my family, in a house that is now a museum in her honor called the Casa Museo Felisa Rincón de Gautier. Everyone knew Doña Fela. She was always outside and available to all, a loving woman to whom people were instantly drawn.

When I was a little girl, she was already in her golden years. Although she was always well-dressed and regal, Doña Fela was never too important for her people, no matter their age. When we wanted swings in the playground, she granted the neighborhood children audience in her office at the city hall. And on hot days when we played near her home, she offered us lemonade.

Doña Fela's kindness and generosity were contagious. My father and first art teacher, Alfonso Arana, gave free outdoor art classes to children on Saturday afternoons. All his students, regardless of where we came from—the Old City or the poor neighborhood of La Perla—would be together drawing and laughing. Breaking down socioeconomic barriers was at the core of Doña Fela's beliefs and politics.

Like the beautiful island of Puerto Rico, my art is full of color and warmth. Painting brings me joy, and being able to contribute to the already existing beauty in this world is incredibly rewarding. The time spent researching, sketching, and illustrating this picture book brought back so many memories of being a little girl in awe of such a grand, strong, and fierce woman.

I always felt affection for Doña Fela, but the more research I did, the more I appreciated what a visionary she was for her time and how much she did for the Puerto Rican people.